THE DEAD CAN'T DANCE

THE DEAD
CAN'T DANCE

Pam Calabrese MacLean

RONSDALE PRESS

THE DEAD CAN'T DANCE
Copyright © 2009 Pam Calabrese MacLean

All rights reserved. No part of this publication may be reproduced, stored in a retrieval system, or transmitted, in any form or by any means, without prior written permission of the publisher, or, in Canada, in the case of photocopying or other reprographic copying, a licence from Access Copyright (Canadian Copyright Licensing Agency).

RONSDALE PRESS
3350 West 21st Avenue
Vancouver, B.C., Canada V6S 1G7
www.ronsdalepress.com

Typesetting: Julie Cochrane, in New Baskerville 11 pt on 13.5
Cover Design: David Drummond
Author Photo: Suzanne van den Hoogen
Paper: Ancient Forest Friendly Silva — 100% post-consumer waste, totally chlorine-free and acid-free

Ronsdale Press wishes to thank the following for their support of its publishing program: the Canada Council for the Arts, the Government of Canada through the Book Publishing Industry Development Program (BPIDP), and the Province of British Columbia through the Book Publishing Tax Credit Program and the British Columbia Arts Council.

Library and Archives Canada Cataloguing in Publication

MacLean, Pam, 1950–
    The dead can't dance / by Pam Calabrese MacLean.

Poems.
ISBN 978-1-55380-069-9

    I. Title.

PS8575.L443D42 2009   C811'.54   C2009-903919-2

At Ronsdale Press we are committed to protecting the environment. To this end we are working with Markets Initiative (www.oldgrowthfree.com) and printers to phase out our use of paper produced from ancient forests. This book is one step towards that goal.

Printed in Canada by Marquis Book Printing, Quebec, Canada

For Donard
(1949–2008)

So speak to me again, my friend.
Tell me how we danced the world away
one slow step at a time.

ACKNOWLEDGEMENTS

Some of the poems in this book were previously published in *Carousel, Concrete Wolf* (US), *Contemporary Verse 2, Dandelion, Grist, Matrix, McGill Street Magazine, New Writer* (UK), *Other Voices, Pottersfield Portfolio, Room, sub-Terrain, The Antigonish Review, White Water Journal,* and *Zygote.* And some have won awards from competitions in *CV2, Matrix, New Writer* (UK), *Room* and *Zygote.*

Special thanks to Anne Simpson and Stephanie Bolster for their words on my words, to Ron Hatch and his appreciation of my words, to my family and friends, good, faithful reader-listeners.

And Dale.

CONTENTS

The Morning You Leave Me

—

Dear John Letter / 13
Everything / 14
The Morning You Leave Me / 15
Stars Will Bend / 16
The Florist / 18
Their Only Grace / 19
Endings / 20
Dream Date / 21
Elevator / 23
Hunter / 24
Together / 25
Do I Still Talk of Love? / 27
Dusk / 28
From the Ocean / 29
Dream House / 30
Larger Than Life / 32
Then Tomorrow / 33
Speak to Me / 34
Sunday / 36

On a Chair Outside the Living

Marshmallows / 39
Dead Man's Flats / 40
The Moves / 41
Fat Kid / 42
My Father / 43
In a Flash / 44
Something Has to Be Done about That Dog / 45
Sorry for Your Loss / 46
Photographs Your Body Takes / 47
The Dead Can't Dance / 48
Midnight / 49
Dream Diner / 50
My Father Is Thirty Years Dead / 54
Small Change / 55
Blindside / 56
Old Home Movies Have My Dead Father Walking Again / 58
My Father Was Full of Birds / 59
Grief / 60

The Ida-Mae Poems

In Strictest Confidence / 63
Penis Envy / 64
Ida-Mae Believes / 65
Overlistening / 66

Calling the Tune / 67
Pet Names / 68
Birthing / 69
Zucchini / 70
Ida-Mae Talks to Her Daughters / 72
Her Father's Barn / 74
Lucy / 76
Upbringing / 79
How Are Ya Now? / 80
Silas Simms / 81
Butter / 83
And There Is Always More Zucchini / 84
Sweet Grass / 85

River

River / 89

Cud

Aubade / 101
Reiki / 102
Part of Me / 103
Footprints on the Sky / 105
Garbage Day on Pine Street / 106
Cud / 107

Design / 109
Before / 110
Like a Cowboy, Shot from His Horse / 111
First Steps / 112
Bus / 114
Planting Spring / 116
Pockets Full of Rotten Oranges / 118
Rearview Mirror / 120
The Scattering / 122
The Smells of Clover / 123
Memory Train / 124
Her Own Strength / 126
Stones / 127
All the Way Over / 128

About the Author / 131

The Morning You Leave Me

—

*I approach love
the way a cow crosses ice.
Body held tight
legs splayed in loose invitation
nose to ground
sniffing out the glib joke,
wanting only to lie down,
get it over.*

Dear John Letter

Dear John,

I need to speak plainly.
Write you a small poem
before the words get in the way,
the light gets in my eyes,
you under my skin.

I need to tell you,
not that I am leaving
but rather
that I am gone.

Look up.

No words on my tongue;
no light in my eyes;
nothing under this woman skin.

Nothing left of me

but you.

Everything

I remember everything
I've ever killed.

The details remain
like fingerprints,
mine and only mine.

The seagull on my windshield;

the mouse under my wheels;

three hornets that brought my son
screaming from sleep;

the crow I only meant to scare
with the gun I got for Christmas;

the injured rabbit because he asked.

And love.

Always love.

The Morning You Leave Me

The morning you leave me,
I'll breakfast on a snowy field
violent with berries.
I'll stuff my mouth,
swallow you.

I'll eat my way back
to the first time
I held you
on my tongue.
The sudden sweet surprise
of strawberries
one winter afternoon.

Then delicately,
as if the stains
belong on another's lips,
another's fingertips,
I'll begin to pick
at my own flesh.

Stars Will Bend

I gather beach glass
hold it in my open hand,
tell you of the girl who hides
where seagulls roost in trees.
How she has made these marks,
etched them deep.
Sent us her cry for help.

And you, so very patient, speak to me of sea and sand
and how time writes itself everywhere.

After father died
I brought a photograph
that showed him standing
next to you, a witness
to his own burial,
his hand gesturing heavenward,
his smile open as the grave
and just for you.

And you said, *Double exposure*
explained it all to me, as if you had not already tried
a thousand times to teach me to see through magic.

Last night I woke at midnight
to a sky milky green.
I opened the window.
I went outside.
Still it was as if someone had flung
the green green sea.
By morning everything will be different.

Stars will bend,
beneath our feet
and trees will hang
unrooted,
waiting to be wished upon.

And you will have no explanation, no reason on this earth
to love me.

But you will.

The Florist

You never say love
except of bowling,
late night jazz,
brie in puff pastry.

You say I love you
is at best a question,
whose silent reply is feared
almost as much
as the quick and thoughtless
Iloveyoutoo.

That good-mannered excuse-me
to a burp of the heart.

In this we are alike,
you and I.
It is only the florist,
who after so many years,
dares sign your name,
with love.

Their Only Grace

I need to love
a Bartholomew,
a Jedidiah
an Emmanuel.
Need to open my mouth
in all the classic postures of love,
need the long feel on my tongue,
the slow release of syllables.

So far I've loved men
whose names are short
for nothing.
Kent.
Luke.
Kirk.
Quick blunt pokes
of sound.

Their only grace,
how easily I leave them.
These men
whose names already sound
like a door slammed.
Or a face
and an open hand.

Endings

There is an old dog
on my street. I see him everywhere,
hunched and straining.
He belongs to a man
whose wife left him so long ago
he remembers her by another's name.
In the night he cries out, *Olivia, Olivia*
but she was called Amanda.

There are the beginnings of poems
all over town. Every one belongs to you.
I bring them home by the armful,
pack them in an old suitcase
as if there were somewhere
I might take them.

The dog has given up,
is slowly dying
in his own back yard,
but I have learned
his dark, snuffling ways
and walk the streets
hunched and straining
calling out your name
and even when I get it right
I know that endings too,
are everywhere.

See how I step through them
and am lost.

Dream Date

Getting it in the back
booth of the dream diner
from a boy whose name
I won't recall
and when his young friends join us,
with their cherry-cokes,
greasy fries and gravy,
we sit up naked.

One pimple-studded boy points a fry,
says in a voice that surprises even him,
You are bejeweled.
Every kiss,
each brush of lips,
scattered opals on our skin.
And our tongues set them on fire.

I wake middle-aged,
dress my lackluster flesh
young-girl-sluttish and go downtown.
Certain I will know him.
The bars are filled
and at every table,
in every darkened corner,
the talk is of me.

Who can resist a good story about herself?

I linger,
move from one group to another,
once or twice seeing
the dazzle of him
out of the corner of my eye.
By the time I head home,
it's winter
and the moon has laid
stars on the snow.

Elevator

She steps into the elevator,
pushes the button for the floor
she's already on,
and waits.

Wonders why nothing is happening.

Remembers she once had sex in an elevator.
It didn't go anywhere either.

Sees her mistake,
and how like her life it is.
Waiting, nothing happening,
disappointment blinding her
to the fact that she is already
exactly

where she wanted to be.

Hunter

I wanted to be the gun he handled
every Friday night during deer season.
His hands along the barrel, the special oils
and soft rags, the care taken to get it right.
The whole evening the gun in his lap,
the shining caress.

That last fall, he shot a small doe
on his way to work. Gutted her in the field
and splayed her on the hood of his truck.
Drove around like that all day, stopping
at ten gas stations for two dollars worth
while her blood dried on the headlights.

And still needed me
to see her. Hollowed out
and cold, hung from a low rafter,
the wind through the old barn moving
the hair on her ears. Her remaining eye
blind with his image and some small future
the gun raised,
the aim taken
and the long drive home after dark.

Together

Deer had been coming into the orchard for weeks,
sharing the apples with our horses.
I took my coffee out into the still dark
to watch. When the morning shadows showed,
I'd clap my hands, and the horses would stir
and move sleepily toward breakfast.
The deer would sail over the fence. A white wave
goodbye and the wall of trees
opening closing,
quick as an eye.

There were never any deer on Saturday.
His only day to hunt.

He didn't think the deer were clever.
Something must be setting them off. He tried leaving
the horses out on Friday. As if it were any other night
and the orchard safe.
He hid the truck as if he were still away.
Covered his tracks. Tried to think more
like a predator.

Every Saturday he got up a little earlier.

I planned to tell him
as soon as hunting season was over.
I thought we might learn
to laugh about it
together.
How I made sure I was up before him
and hidden
under the apple trees, waiting
for the right moment

to jump out, cotton sacks flapping
wild and white on my outstretched arms.
The frenzied run, the horses' hooves tearing up the earth,
and the deer
frightened to life.

Do I Still Talk of Love?

A week spent
cleaning the library
throwing out the past,
the broken
the redundant
the obsolete.

This morning I walked
through a basement corridor
no longer choked
with chairs, broken metal shelves,
boxes of duplicate *Cosmopolitans*.

For the first time in twenty years
I was uncomfortable there.

How safe
the clutter
of my home
my garden
my life.
So yes,
I still talk of love.

Come Love.
Clutter me.

Dusk

An armless man roars
his Harley past my door
again and again.
A dog with no legs chases him,
holding up a hat and gloves.
A headless woman turns from her flowers
to claim the hat.

Dusk and unlikely things
play themselves out
on Hawthorne Street.

I can easily place you there,
walking home to me,
your day tucked under your arm
or hidden in your briefcase.
I wonder what you've left behind
this time.
And if I can live without it
when dusk turns.

From the Ocean

Now I see where the snow comes from.
The ocean, he tells me.

All day the snow he speaks of,
has whispered down
from a cloudless sky.
Not steady, but brief
white moments.

We stand apart,
looking out over the water
at a swarm of flakes.
He doesn't take his hands
from behind his back.
As I turn away,
I see he's closed his eyes,
tipped his face heavenward.

Ten words.
The first he's spoken since morning
and wanting a divorce.

Dream House

Our house was barely lived in,
the boxes still unpacked.
We made love where the bed would be
and fell asleep.

I dreamed he was in love
with someone else,
couldn't wait for me
to know her.

He pointed out our window
to the farthest spit of land,
where the channel cuts
the harbour deep,
said that's where he'd build
her house.

And would I help?

It might have been summer,
the harbour flat and calm
a thin ribbon of deep water showing the way.
But in the dark of the dream
it was always winter.
An empty page of ice,
as night after night
I carried materials along the shore.
Ever anxious to please.

I awoke crying so often,
angry at him still in my bed,
each time forgetting
there was no other woman,
no other house.

Not being loved by him
began to feel right.
So with every trip
I set aside
a nail
a board
a need
for a house of my own.

Larger Than Life

I saw your husband today.
So strange to see a dead man
driving a small red car.

Most choose sky
blue and larger
than life.

I beckon him
to the curb,
shift the dry flowers
to the back seat.
He drives me home.

He only talks of you.
How pleased he is,
you — moving on so fast.
Finding love
again.

He tells me you gave away
his old recliner and now his dog
sits beside
a different chair, a different hand
and rarely lifts his head expectantly.

He begins to cry
but doesn't speak again
until he's sure I have one foot
on solid ground.

He asks me then:
Do you know him?
Is he anything like me?

Then Tomorrow

I'm going upstairs right now.
Taking all those pills.
But

what if no one notices?

What if they're watching CNN
or flossing their teeth
and

they think
she always falls asleep early in weird places
so

I won't wake her.

Can't wake her.

Then tomorrow

won't be the day
I buy my Christmas tree
from a young man named Hugh

his dumpster dog Herbie
won't sit on my knee
in the cab of an '84 Ford

as he delivers me.
Home.

Speak to Me

What gives memory the right
to come in here
all bright-eyed, eager-breathed,
longing lolling on his tongue?

I thought him locked away,
framed and nailed up
last page of the photo album.
Yet here he is

rollicking toward me
a figure eight through my legs
his hands as if never folded on his breast
his tongue

oh God, the tongue again.

So speak to me.

Tell me about the time
you had to pull over
you so hard against the wheel
there was no steering the damn car.

Tell me the night you waited while I danced
with fifty or was it 100 other men
(so you said it seemed)
until the last dance.

You said then
I will always want to be the last.

So speak to me again, my friend.

Tell me
how we danced the world away
one slow step at a time.

Sunday

Driving up my lane
in how many Friday-night cars,
finding me in one kitchen or another,
the first when I was sixteen,
the last just yesterday
if we count the flesh of memory.

Forty years
you staying away each time I married,
each time you fell in love.

They said you were waiting for me,
and without you, I'd never be happy.

Seems we could have made a lot of people happy,
my children, your sisters.
Even my mother thought
we should marry.

Thank God we knew Sunday,
your tail lights
disappearing around the last turn,
both of us already somewhere else,
each forgetting,
in our own way
to wave.

On a Chair Outside the Living

—

The dead don't celebrate
birthdays,
their candles snuffed
or broken.
So tonight I'll light my father
one of mine,
keep it from draft
and death.
I'll cry out,
and he'll come.

Marshmallows

Roasting marshmallows
reminds me of my father.

My father caught fire
between the time I got to school and
first bell. His soft insides
smouldered for days,
trapped in his crisp skin.

While others watched his kidneys,
I was made to wait
at home,
at school,
at church.
Kidneys are the worst,
they told me.

In the end it was his heart.

Dead Man's Flats

We get off the bus in Dead Man's Flats.
Looking for my father.
We'd kept our eyes open,
all across the country,
watching for signs.
Everything pointed here.

We sit by the river
and my mother reconstructs
his big toes poking through his socks,
hands, the size of stop signs,
his blind eye.
His flesh she draws out in stories.

We are so close to finding him.

She even tells me how they'd made love
the first time,
their wedding night.
Upper berth of a west-bound train.

I'm certain I was there too.
My father's arms a charmed circle
where my mother and I slept,
lulled and unsuspecting.
Even then, on our way
to Dead Man's Flats.

The Moves

I was always in the room,
learning the moves.
Watching the grade twelve boys,
perfect as marble pieces,
play chess.
They never spoke
my name.

My father did two things that year.
He taught me to play chess.
Slowly and intricately.
His rough hands gentle as he talked of choices,
limitations, respect for spaces
where we do not belong.

And he died.

Fat Kid

No matter what disguise
I ferret out, I am still
the fat kid in wool jodhpurs, thighs
chafed raw.
Daddy's little girl,
squinting at the February sky, losing
his face in the sun.
Another red balloon floating free.

I am still the inattentive dreamer, caught
forever unaware, slack fingered, too late
grasping at bits of string, left
holding nothing,
surprised by the weight of it.

My Father

had six eyes
one good,
four that laid at rest, unblinking,
with his starched hankies
in a cedar box.
And he had a best eye,
also the newest.
Hand-painted but unsigned, it had
no license to move.
Just filled the empty socket
so people could meet him honestly.

In a Flash

Dying took nine days
from his catching fire to his
heart's burning up in a flash
not bright enough to
pale the February stars
but still
it woke me
hours before my mother
said, *Your father's gone.*

Christmas came
quick as any child could wish
and back from church,
my Mom and I,
not knowing how to fill this house
where he had never lived,
opened all our gifts.
They were many
and fine and wasted.
No miracles
from God or Santa Claus.

Christmas was
like his leaving,
too small,
too quiet.
Just a father
gone to work,
forever.

Something Has to Be Done about That Dog

The dog sits at the end of our lane,
late afternoon, day after day.
His tail lifts dust as each of the men
pass, shifting their lunch cans,
hard hats, eyes.

The dog doesn't come home,
even after all the doors are closed,
and the men have finished their suppers,
pushed back from their tables,
without mentioning my father.
The accident.
They talk instead about the dog.
How something has to be done.

I go down the lane, rehearsing
how I'll grab him,
shake him, yell,
He's dead, you stupid animal.
He left you
and he's not coming back.
Ever.

Instead, I spread my jacket,
sit on it in the grass.
And the dog, cold now,
climbs into my lap.

Sorry for Your Loss

You lose
        recipes
        books
        stamps
        games
        chances
        your driver's licence

You do not lose the dead.

I dug my father's grave
                lowered him
                covered him
                weighed him down
                wrote it in stone

And know forever
                where he is.

Photographs Your Body Takes

Jerry and my father
were the fixed points
I travelled to and from
every Friday night.

Dad would drop me off
and I'd dance all evening with the other girls
too young to be in cars
with boys.

Last dance was "Whiter Shade of Pale"
and saved for Jerry,
his body woven in and out of mine
in places my body hardly knew.

He'd waltz me to the door, leave me
to stand alone on the Legion stairs
until Dad flicked the lights and I'd walk
through my own breath to the car.

Forty years they've remained connected.

"Whiter Shade" still frames them,
still moves Jerry's leg between my thighs.
And keeps my father
outside the dance.
Waiting.

The Dead Can't Dance

The dead can't dance
their daughters
to that place above,
or the time before
the torn and open earth.
Or anywhere at all.

Oh, they remember
the tiny face,
and want to know again
the weight of love lifted high.
But their arms are dust
and someone has buried their shoes.

Midnight

In dreams,
I know my lover
with my eyes closed.
His lips ripen.
He sweats
and grunts,
while my father
sits patiently,
on a chair outside
the living.

I bury my father,
fresh each night,
plan his funeral supper,
a feast,
a banquet,
a table
I alone
leave hungry.

Dream Diner

A sign outside the diner
tells me every morning now
that my father's been here,
cooking, waiting
on the dead for thirty years.

It took a long time to find him.

That first morning I walked in
with the *Help Wanted* sign under my arm
he was pulling plump gray pigeons
from the rafters over his head.
He'd slice down the breast with his nail,
insert both thumbs and peel back
the feathered skins like tiny hooded coats
before he popped the pigeons squawking into the hot fat.
Their small voices followed me down the hallway
where I found buckets, rags and oily cleanser.

I began scrubbing the red leather booths.

He won't let me clean the booth
at the very back.
I sneak glimpses of the photograph
beside the plastic flowers.
It's my mother all right.
A layer of grease and the words,
Reserved for my love,
paper-clipped to the picture
keep the booth empty all the time.

I wonder that she's not here yet.

I remember being here when all three of us
were living. I was a child and my mother and I
were dressed in white Viyella. Matched. Except her suit
had the hand print of a hot iron on the shoulder
and mine had box pleats.
They were trying to decide which one of them
should die and afraid they'd ask me to choose,
I bounced up and down up and down
up and down in my black and white oxfords
until the leather seat began to crack. My mother yelled.
I stuck out my tongue. She pinched my inner thigh and we
were suddenly home. The decision made.

—

Jewels of ketchup edge each plate
surround the lump of pigeon on its nest
of carrot curls, pronged celery.
My father spit-shines every plate,
Nothing like it, he says buffing with his apron.

The dead don't care about any of it.
They come here for his stories. He's the youngest,
has come freshest from the living.
Has not forgotten the hot smell of asphalt
or a woman's crotch, pointy breasts
or the high round ones that feel
like worlds in your hands. Still knows
all the dance steps and how it feels
when a woman thinks she loves you and the weight
of a child draped over your shoulders, her candied fingers
in your hair. Still remembers living.

Just wait till your living start showing up here, he tells them
looking at me for the first time. *You think it's what you want.
But when everyone you remember gets here, there's no one to remember.*

He asks me to dance but I notice someone has taken his
shoes and the pigeons fly down from the rafters, agitated,
and the dead are all talking at once, offering their shoes,
until one by one they discover that theirs too have been
buried or passed on.

—

My father dances
barefoot
through cigarette butts,
pigeon droppings.
He tries once
or twice to toss me up
in some barely remembered game
but he is suddenly all
ashes and misery.
He drops me, goes out back for a smoke.

I'm left to face the dead
who no longer sway to the music
and have just spotted my shoes.

That's how I know I'm not dead. The oxfords.

—

He follows me home that night,
steps cautiously, unsure of how things
have been arranged in his absence.
He keeps one step behind me
down into the basement, squats off to my right,
as I feed the stove. We watch the flames
for a while. I feel him crawl along my shoulders,
warming them. A dead father's embrace
lugged through childhood like a cumbersome,
sook-worn blanket.

He could be a guardian angel.

We stay like this for days. Before he leaves,
he tells me not to come back to the diner.
Doesn't want to see me there again.
The dead have their dreams too, he whispers
closing the door.

When I'm sure the house is empty,
I retrace our steps,
smash the glass door of the diner.
Set the pigeons free.

My Father Is Thirty Years Dead

My therapist wants me to build a room.
I do the whole downstairs.
Walls, windows, floor-to-ceiling shelves,
framed photographs, narrow archway,
upright piano, louvered doors.

I'm supposed to say, "Come in."
And wait to see who does.

My father is the only guest.
He walks toward me in his Sunday suit,
his hat, his scarf, his gloves.
Death has changed nothing.

He removes his hat as he always did.
With his thumb on one side of the crown,
three fingers on the other,
his index finger in the dent on top,
he plucks it from his head,
tosses it lightly.

He has not lost his touch
and his hat strikes the wall
in just the right spot,
at just the right angle.

But I've forgotten the hooks
and his hat rolls to a stop at my feet.

Small Change

The Change Game was my father's.
He'd take all his pennies,
nickels, dimes and quarters,
shake them in his hands
before giving me a quick peek.
If I guessed close enough,
the money was mine.

I got so good at it,
that even now, forty years later,
the jingling of coins
shows me their image
against my father's palm.
I see them so clearly,
I can count them.

Nickels imitating quarters,
dimes barely visible,
pennies bunched on his life line.
It's my father's face
I've spent,
carelessly,
like so much small change.

Blindside

When I was very young, my father did shift work. He walked home from the plant through the silent field where we played baseball daytime. He'd get home about 12:30. Mom always left a lunch on the table. While Dad boiled water for tea, he'd take out his glass eye and wrap it in a kleenex. Home is where you can do things like that. Two days after Dad got his first hand-painted eye, Mom accidentally threw the kleenex and the eye in the coal stove. That was before I was born. She left a lunch then too.

I'd leave things on the table for Dad. Broken things. A doll with a missing leg, an eye stuck open or closed. A snapped barrette. I remember a favourite one with turtles on it, four of them, a red, a yellow, a blue and a green. It broke right through the middle of the blue.

I see him sitting there, in the half dark. He was always in the half dark. His hands were big and clumsy but he'd work and curse these small unmanageable accidents. Always ready by morning, the repairs hidden.

Later the things he fixed could not be left on the table. They were secrets shared late at night. Boys I liked, boys I hated. He'd tell me what I needed to know. He'd close his good eye if the going got too rough.

He was here last night, sitting at my table. I wasn't expecting him, so at first I saw only the table. Filled. Dirty dishes, a pile of unpaid bills, a broken doll. Dad watched as I cleared away the remains of supper, wrote cheques and sealed them in envelopes. Finding stamps took a while. He never moved or asked for anything. He marvelled at the finality of crazy glue, though he didn't say it.

I didn't know what else to do, so I made tea. Hot and black.
I couldn't even remember if he liked milk. I placed the cup
on his good side and asked if he remembered how he'd
caught my reflection in the kettle and pretended his glass eye
could always see me. No matter where he might be. But he
seemed slow to remember. The dead often are.

Suddenly I knew he'd grown tired of this visit. I gathered
him like the bones of dead birds and laid him on my bed.
I combed his hair and washed his face before I closed his eye.
I thought I should go to the garden. Get handfuls of earth.

Old Home Movies Have My Dead Father Walking Again

I was saving to buy a horse
the year this movie was taken.
Instead I bought Dad the camera.
Every time he told someone I'd said,
There goes the ass-end off my horse,
he'd laugh, just the way he's doing now
on my living room wall. Head thrown back.
His hands trapped in his pockets.

I miss the sound of him.

Now I see he is talking
as he walks. His mouth moves easily
around words I strain to hear.
I need just one.

So intent on being a good girl,
listening this time, I forget
who's running the show. Cracks appear
in the grass and sky. Light leaks
through my father.
I wait for the empty square to tell me
we've reached the end.

My Father Was Full of Birds

If I were a photographer
I would not advance the film
but stay that child of five
on my father's knee
in our sky-blue dodge,
Mom driving,
Dad doing bird songs.

And when he laughed,
I'd hold his mouth
open.
See each bird nesting,
deep in him.

But the photo disappoints,
shows only my hands
caught in the air.
His face fading.

Better a painter.
More control.
I could hold us living
in unexpected colours,
fill the air with wings.

Lay my brushes down.
Turn
and walk away.

Grief

Grief is not finger food
to be taken
in small measured bites.
Do that and you eat
your whole life
stale and bitter.

Rather stuff your mouth,
wipe the excess away
and gorge again.
Swallow
and swallow
and swallow.

Then wait
on appetite,
and when it comes
ten, a hundred
one thousand times ravenous:

Pray
it comes for joy.

The Ida-Mae Poems

—

*There I was alone with a choice,
that was no choice at all.
I put one foot in front of the other
Six thousand, six hundred and thirty-six times,
following my life up that lane.*

In Strictest Confidence

The closest Ida-Mae ever came
to an opinion on the country
was something she said
in strictest confidence to old Maud Purcell,
who just, by the way,
told all 2,219 residents
here and about.

Maud said,
Ida-Mae says
She's wantin' to marry
a loose-tongued,
long-fingered,
city man.

Maud said,
Ida-Mae says
No tongue-tied,
snub-nosed,
blunt-fingered,
country bumpkin
is ever gonna rub her the wrong way.

Penis Envy

Raised with five brothers
Ida-Mae was twelve before
she realized she was not deformed.
And almost thirteen
before she knew
she'd been blessed.

Ida-Mae Believes

the size
and angle of decline
of a man's nose
is
directly proportional
and
in direct opposition
to
the size
and angle of incline
of that man's erect penis.

This accounts for a great deal
of Ida-Mae's face gazing.

Overlistening

Six years of being
married to Angus and his
I'm-gonna-do-this-no-matter-what lust
left Ida-Mae barren, fidgety
and overlistening
to Maud Purcell and Bernice Bates on the phone.
Maud was saying,
Well ya know, Bernice,
Pa always sayed
if ya can't get a mare in foal —
change the stud.
Ida-Mae hoots and slams the phone,
does a little dance.

Maud-Bernice was born nine months later
(give or take the few days it took Ida-Mae
to find the perfect stud).

Calling the Tune

Believing
under the apple trees
is for cows
meant Angus married Ida-Mae,
indoors, in July.
Hot, sticky, wet and tired.

Ida-Mae feared Angus
would forever call the tune,
and she would dance.
Days and nights and days,
blistered feet and more,
aching for a slow turn.

Sure enough,
Angus did call the tune,
had most to do with
hot, sticky, wet and tired
but nothing,
nothing save the fiddling,
to do with the first eight of
Ida-Mae's nine children.

Pet Names

Ida-Mae has pet names
for all her lovers,
helps keep straight
who belongs to who.
On each child's birthday
Ida-Mae spends time
remembering the father.

She chuckles
over her last lover,
Catherine-Billy's dad.
Ida-Mae nick-named him
Bungalow Bill
nothing upstairs
but Lord, the basement.

Birthing

Angus's plumped eyeballs roll madly
around the room. He looks once
at the straining Ida-Mae,
her huge feet hanging in the air.
Her head appears
grimacing between her legs.

After each contraction
Ida-Mae tries to catch
even one eye, smooth his breathing.
Angus is half-way to the door
when Emma spills into the room.
He turns and takes her in,
settles easy.

Ida-Mae holds the sight of them,
clear and sharp,
roots and wings.
Sees all that Angus has let go.
And in that moment
between birthing and sleep,
she can almost forgive him,
her mistakes.

Zucchini

Why do townies lock their cars in the fall?
Keep them from filling up with zucchini!

Angus's perennial joke.
Ida-Mae is the one
drives around town trying
to give the stuff away.
Two hours of side-streets, main-streets,
dead-ends, before she spots a prairie licence plate.
The car is fire-engine red
and the doors are O P E N.

Ida-Mae gets caught red-handed
by Red-Hughie, whose hair matches his car.
City boy, not too familiar
with zucchini.
He gets all of Ida-Mae's
and come spring, Angus,
gets the son he wanted.

Ida-Mae was a little bit
in love. Didn't think
it through this time.
Didn't even try to match
Red-Hughie's features with the features
of the fathers
of Angus's other children.
Never once figured
on William Xavier
being born with his head on fire
and freckles.

Angus's prize cow had done the same thing last year:
produced a calf the colour of which
Angus couldn't figure.
Ida-Mae knew all along
the neighbour's bull was what happened.
But in Angus's heart
that cow was above suspicion
and on the strength of her strange calf
so was Ida-Mae.

Ida-Mae Talks to Her Daughters

I

There are two kinds of men.
Those who want sex
and those (jerking her thumb
toward the graveyard)
who don't.

II

Home early from school Catherine-Billy bang crashes
her way to the kitchen, jolting Ida-Mae
from her lonely struggle to reach the bottom of the cup.
Ida-Mae thinks her daughter may explode, so she takes
the crumpled paper from Catherine-Billy's shaking fist,
and reads out loud.

THE 1881 STATUTES OF THIS COUNTRY CANADA
DEFINE DISABLED PERSONS AS ANY INFANT, LUNATIC,
IDIOT OR MARRIED WOMAN.

Brilliant, says Ida-Mae.
MOM! says Catherine-Billy.
Ida-Mae wishes for time enough
to let Catherine-Billy figure it herself
but she hears the kids getting off the bus.
Think about it, Billy darlin'. They're tellin'
what we should already know —
a woman doesn't have a disability
till she marries one.

III
After fourteen years on their couch
Maud-Bernice's Arnold stood up,
right in the middle of Oprah,
adjusted his privates,
put his ball-hat on sideways,
and walked out.
For good.

Maud started crying in the pickles.
Ida-Mae laid a hand on her daughter's arm.
Wait a bit, girl, you'll see.
No man in your life
is a damn sight better
than no life in your man.

IV
So you think you're in love?
When you see him
your face gets hot.
Can't catch
your breath.
You're dizzy,
your hands sweat.
You get goose bumps.

Listen to me, girl,
these feelings of yours
are the exact same thing
small animals feel
when they're about
to be eaten.

Her Father's Barn

Ida-Mae liked to go there on her own
or with her Ma. Warm eggs secreted in her winter coat,
smells of hay and birth and new milk.
Ida-Mae would always ask
why fathers were kept to themselves
and wonder at how sad her mother's smile could be.

She remembers the first time of men there,
five of them, hard and hurried,
come for the birthing. Remembers them sweat
and grunt till the cotton rope lay
slick and bloody at their feet.
Remembers the black calf,
warm and dead.
Hears her own scream, *You bastards got no right,*
feels her father's hand jerk her face around,
It is how it is girl, now git.

Late at night Ida-Mae made secret trips
to listen and watch. Safe,
as darkness tucked in.
Her father ruined it.
Caught her there.
Drove off all her senses
with his own.
Afterwards, she thought about driving
the pitchfork into her leg,
blaming her father,
telling her mother,
but she guessed her mother already knew
about men
and wounds that never come to scars.

Ida-Mae still finds herself there.
Late at night she waits outside
in the circle from the new electric light
until she calms every shadow.
It's her husband's barn now
and her Pa's dead twenty years.
Still, she crosses herself, spits
and shivering steps in.

Lucy

This dress is the only
decent thing I got
to wear when I'm nursin'
and Lord knows
I'm always nursin'.
It buttons up the front.
Easy access.
I'm tired of that too.
Seems like
my whole damn life
someone's been tryin' to get
somethin' off me,
squeezin' past the last drop of
whatever I got worth havin'.

Well I'm dry,
'cept for forty bucks
I kept a hide.
Gonna buy a new dress —
one I can hardly get into myself.

I get to town walkin' and
on the whole God-forsakin' street
there's no one save me and
some bag lady,
with a dress fits worse than mine.
We walk to meet,
gunslingers,
her with two left boots,
one flat, other well-healed.
I start into shootin' right off.
Yes
I got money

me
Ida-Mae
I saved it and
no one
not Angus
not kids
and for sure
not some damn charity case
is gonna get it.

Her aim's better.
Shoots me
quick and easy with
her dead dog eyes
and limps past.

Shakes me up that look.
I go for a coffee at the 5 to a Dollar,
check the safety pin in my bra, pat the money.

Ermaline, who works the counter says,
"That old woman's pathetic.
Blew in last week and they say
her whole family got burnt up.
She was off somewhere drinking.
They say she carries their bones,
what's left anyway, around in a paper sack.
Been doin' it for years.
Two days past the old fool
loses the bag 'tween here and the post office.
Been beatin' a path there to here,
here to there since. And the old fool stinks."

I go outside to wait.
I shove the forty bucks
right at her, hatin' her then
for being sensical enough to take it.

That money disappears faster
than a snake into a stone wall.
She grabs my arm and
starts back for the post office.
We go slow,
searchin',
pokin' at garbage,
shakin' hedges,
cryin' one time when we
find the wrong bag.
I know it sounds desperate sad
but I was startin' to feel real good.

Dark comes
and we keep on
right past Ermaline
gawkin' out the shop door,
down the road, between the houses,
across the stubbly fields,
past Angus,
gawkin' out the barn door and
right up to the house.
I'm anxious to get in. She stops
me on the top step
and says "Name's Lucy"
and slips that wad of twos
into the pocket of my dress.
I push open the door,
shout We're home,
though I never am sure
which one of us needed the tellin'.

Upbringing

The phone
wakes Ida-Mae
and she pads bare-foot
down to the kitchen.
It's Doc Clayton,
calling middle of the night
for consent. Minor surgery.
It seems Ida-Mae's son, John-Angus,
and his date, Sylvie Bates,
are stuck.
Foreskin cruelly skewered
on her almost perfect
barb-wire teeth.

Sylvie's mother, Bernice,
grabs the phone from Doc Clayton,
takes Ida-Mae to task
for "the touch-and-go upbringing of that
cocky bastard John-Angus."

*Now Bernice, be thankful
your girl was with a boy had sense
enough to save his own skin.*

A thin scream comes back.

*Bernice Bates, you know it had to be
John-Angus did the callin'.
We wouldn't expect a child of yours
to talk with her mouth full,
now would we?*

How Are Ya Now?

Angus uses that phrase
as a "pay attention, woman"
at the beginning of
every encounter.
And at the end
just to let Ida-Mae know
he's done.

It's particularly bad
in the bedroom where
Angus announces his lust
with a "HOWAREYANOW?"
and before Ida-Mae
can answer
he's asking again.

Silas Simms

Folks could easy live without me, but dyin' is different. Angus says that I'm the darlin' of the funeral parlour.

Folks think I got the gift. That no matter how sour the cream I can manage at least one good thing from it. And I always tell it true.

The more off the cream, the more spectators cram the wake house. It's not respect for dead or living. They're waitin' to see me stuck for words or caught up in a lie.

I usually go to a wake on the first day so as not to hold people up. But Silas Simms was given me trouble. Well into the third day when Angus, "Come on Ida-Mae! Can't keep Silas from the devil forever."

The wake house and the bingo hall are one and the same so I'm feelin' some pressure. Bernice Bates, head of the Bingo-for-Jesus group has called three times already. They're right worried Silas won't have gone over by Saturday.

And it's August and hot. Everybody jammed tight and sweaty into that windowless basement. No flowers to cover up — I tell a lie! There is one floral tribute. Silas's mother. Angus thinks she's so old she don't remember what a bastard she gave birth to, but I think she knew what she was doing. It's a wrong-side up horseshoe made of red roses with GOOD LUCK, SON in gold foil. I think she's laughing all Silas' luck pourin' out.

Hardest for me is the widow, my best friend, Audrey. She knows what a bastard Silas was and how much better things are gonna be. He drank the food out of their mouths, gambled away their firewood, beat them all, wife, kids. Threw his old mother downstairs one time. There's some that say he even worried his sheep.

Audrey can't imagine me findin' anything good to say about Silas. Never mind somethin' he was best at. Truth told, I'm wondering too.

Can't get myself straight, fidgetin', can't breathe right. My girdle's too tight and I can hear the whole room "hush-shushing, here she is" by the time I reach the door. Steppin' through I feel like Moses partin' the Red Sea.
Goes so quiet, you could hear a tick swallow.

Audrey's waitin' by the horseshoe. Someone's righted it, so what little luck Silas has left will stay put, but now the letters are upside-down. Audrey's wound so tight her ears are restin' on her shoulders.

I take her hands in mine and I say, "Audrey dear," and I don't bother to whisper, "Audrey dear, there's no one could smoke a cigarette as fast as himself."

Butter

Some nights Angus comes
in from the barn
so horny
even his feet are swollen.

Ida-Mae follows
the manured boots
that track his intentions
through the house.

Nights like these
she disposes of Angus quickly.
Butter should churn
so fast.

Actually,
Ida-Mae prefers butter
It's softer, less clingy
and you almost always have something
to show for your time.

And There Is Always More Zucchini

William Xavier is nearly fifteen,
and Ida-Mae still dreams of sex
with Red-Hughie. It's always fall
and everything's great
till they get down
to the meat and potatoes.
At that moment Red-Hughie's penis
becomes an over-ripe zucchini.
Ida-Mae wakes empty,
wondering
if she and Angus
have put by enough
to last the winter.

Sweet Grass

Braiding sweet grass
with hands that every year
betray her more.

And remembering Emma-Lucille,
hair just that shade of dust
and full of the north wind.

Braided every morning,
Emma wriggling
under Ida-Mae's flying fingers.

And always those braids out straight
chasing after Angus,
who she loved most of all.

Ida-Mae never did get it clean
after the men dragged Emma,
dead, from the manure pit.

It's the little things, Ida-Mae thinks,
that in the end break your heart.
Like sweet grass,
strewn across the winter floor.

River

—

*This morning's river —
dark as a small town lie.*

River

January 13
I stand on the bridge,
lean farther than usual.
My boots halfway to the top rail
on the ledge of last night's snow
prompt a passerby to touch
my shoulder and ask,
Are you OK?

January 14
This morning's river:
a black wound that the ice and snow
try to knit together.

Evening, heading home
and from a different bridge
I can almost see
around the same bend
I can almost see around
from my morning bridge.
What stretch,
what timing would it take
for me to catch myself there
from here?

January 15
A small dark shadow
bubbles along
just under the edge
of new ice, barely visible.
I can think of nothing
but small furtive deaths
and smaller lives.
Already it's that kind of day.

January 16, Morning
—20 Celsius!
Snowing diamonds
over the river
where the sun slides through
the too-still trees —
a breath of wind
and they'd snap
like twigs.

It feels as if nothing
survived the night.

January 16, Evening
The river mimics me,
hat pulled down
scarf up
and the world racing by
its eyes.

January 17
I missed the river this morning,
held my breath,
drove over it
in a wink.
Regret was with me
all day.
Not constant but more
the prick
of the odd pin my mother left,
like conscience,
in the newly hemmed skirts
of my childhood.
Pain surprising me.

I thought I might go at noon
or walk home that way —
the evening trek
on the morning bridge —
just to know if last night's
−30 zipped the river
shut.

But what can this evening's river
tell me of this morning's?

There are footprints
on the river this evening.
A simple dance
of death —
two sets becoming one
where the snow is hollowed
and pink.

The river will hoard
these tracks, keep them
buried under several days
of strange, erratic weather
hold them frozen
open — as if there were still
a chance.

First warm day
they'll rise
out of the old snow
ghosts,
of white on white.

For a moment
before the river opens,
swallows them,
there is hope.

January 20
A workman is positioning his truck
to block the sidewalk.
I walk on
determined
not to understand him,
not to be kept from the river.
With a dirty look,
he moves the truck
to let me past
and I see water
racing along the street,
over the bridge.

The road is river
the river
almost road:
snow-covered
centre line bare-
ly visible,
more shadow than reality
this blue secret life
the river keeps.

January 21
This evening I decide
to cross both bridges.
Not, of course, at the same time.
Though
I can't help wondering,
if I could, would I
cross both
in same direction
or walk to meet myself
a span of river
in between.

January 22
The river is abandoning me,
closing itself,
all the more seductive
for what it covers.

A little vow
of water
remains open
near the far shore.

The winds are high
and suddenly at my feet
a seed pod,
fingernail size,
wings
of old brown leaves.
And another in the snow,
and another,
running down the slope
to the river.
Tiny survivors,
their arms flailing,
heads barely kept
above the snow,
and such a long, long way
to go.

January 24
The river feigns death,
one eye left
open to the world.

After dark I sneak back,
unexpected.
My first night visit.
And maybe it *is* the water —
beneath a clear strip
of ice, under the curling bank of snow —
that catches the light
throws it back
eerie blue.
But I think
alone
deep in its darkened house,
not wanting to answer the door,
the river is watching
TV.

January 27
The river is open and carving
what must feel like
a new geography,
miniature icebergs giving way
lick by lick
and I want to say
this will come to nothing
new
but the river races on,
lost in excitement.

And I suppose given enough time
the river does change
things.

January 31
This morning's river —
dark as a small town lie.

February 14
Blue snow, unrelenting cold
silent
save the soft slide of the river
and the occasional CRACK
of the heart
wood.

March 27
So much water
under the bridge
in my absence.
Who says it can never come again?
Perhaps, like the past
it returns
unrecognized.

What if we could mark the past?
Tag it like the monarch butterfly,
the Canada goose,
the lemming.
Would we learn
to do things differently?

March 28
The river has forgotten
its place.
Or lost its way.
It drifts along footpaths,
squirrels up the trunks
of trees, hoping
for a vantage point.

April 3
Teardrops of ice
the size of light bulbs
dangle from a dead branch
over the river.
They sway back and forth
like young boys
on a diving board,
agitated,
almost ready
to take the plunge.

May 5
The river came to me
last night
flowing through my yard
under the ash
tree that grew 100 years
overnight.
The sun and a full
moon and the river
in between.

Oh, I wish I knew
what it meant.
What I'm supposed to learn.

Then I see this is my dream,
for there I am
facing myself
across the river.
And oh, so human,
I can't remember why
this was ever what I wanted.

Cud

—

The distant square of pasture
is the velvet green
lining of an old game box,
tucked in the back of my childhood
closet. The black and white cows,
jumbled in the far corner,
the forgotten pawns.

Aubade

So still this morning.

Perhaps it was my opening
the door that hushed the world.
Not even bird song
and I swear I heard the magnolia
drop that first petal,
its quiet back-and-forth breath
down through the air,
the gasp as it met the earth.

Then as if at a maestro's stroke
the world began again: cats
on the deck, night-lean and hungry;
birds about their business,
single-minded,
as only birds can be;
the milk truck rattling by.

The baby stirs,
I see for a moment
from beneath her closed eyes
how right it all is.

Reiki

Hands hovering above me
she says once again,
that I am apple blossoms and talks of them
until they fill the room.

I drift down
through the old orchard,
shovel in hand to where the dog waits,
his favourite blanket,
a simple shroud.

At dusk, lightning
rips a limb from the tree.

I hold my breath through the long winter,
until the lump in snow
becomes a small warm body,
waiting.

It blooms in spring, bears fruit
which I gather at dusk
in a wind that mimics the dog's voice.

I know now what to do,
drag the limb to the wood pile.
First bite of the axe
sets us both free.

Part of Me

Part of me is there
in the west coast sun
5:00 a.m.
the street sweeper going by.

Part of me is breakfasting with a blue-gray parrot
who gave me the twice over
and thought me enough.

Part of me is standing
in the stark February light
at my father's open grave.

Part of me is pushing my sons out
one two three
into the world.

Part of me watches
my youngest
watching his daughter's head
crown.

Watches too as he packs up
his toys to make room
in his childhood for her.

Part of me lies still
with my lover, the study of his body
a lifetime.

Tomorrow, part of me will be here
where just now,
impossible as it seems,
all of me is with you
offering up
the only prayers I know.

Footprints on the Sky

I push her on the swing in the back yard, her pant legs sliding
up to reveal her mismatched socks, her sneakers reaching
reaching to leave footprints on the sky.

And every time as her toes clear the tip of the old tree,
never mind the rolling hills, the country roads,
the miles of lane in between,
she says, *I can see Grand-dad's barn.*

I used to be able to see that far.

I walked early this morning,
discovering the garden again,
remembering how the old cat would drink the drops of water
cupped overnight in the Lady's Mantle.

I am, for one moment, allowed my grand-daughter's eyes
and the gift of memory's cat,
his tongue, no less pink,
swallowing world after green and perfect world.

Garbage Day on Pine Street

There's a dead cat
on your street, she tells me.
Looks like he's sleeping.
Could be yours.

I know exactly how he looks,
stretched out long
right down the middle.

Racing home,
I find a marmalade cat in a tree,
alive
and someone else's.
And a mound of orange
that is only earth and leaves.

It's garbage day on Pine
and there are so many boxes
just the right size.
I search through them all.

He's home before I am,
impatient for his lunch.
And hollowed by the particular
and certain grief of him,
I have no defence
against this crippling joy.

Cud

I am a creature of habit.
The woman understands this
to be other than virtue or vice.
It is simple fact.
In no way does it give her cause
to think of me as a being of lesser brain or heart.
She never rushes me.
Always lets me take the long way to the well.
I test her patience some mornings
but she only stands and watches, smiling.
I always hurry then.

Some of my habit I share with her.
Frame her day neatly,
between morning and evening milkings.
She comes again late at night.
This time I like the best.
She asks little of me but my company.
As she works, she speaks of things
most cows are never privy to,
although we understand them well enough.
She shovels and gives fresh hay and water
and armfuls of clean straw.
Just before she leaves, she brushes my face.

I grow old.
There will be no more brindle calves.
This bothers her so much more than it does me.
But she is a practical woman, with a family to feed.
She will eat me.

I have not known her to shirk.
One summer I nearly tore off a teat.
Milking that quarter was out of the question.
Twice a day she inserted a straw in the milk duct,
crying for me the whole time.
I felt only relief.

My dying will be much the same.
I will be relieved and she will cry.
She will not fill my stall quickly.
This pleases me.
For I am a creature of habit
and may not know where else to be.

Design

I like spiders,
watch for them,
mindful of how hard
we both work.
One I know well.
She looks at me
as if she believes
I too know why I'm here.

Last night I wrecked her web.
To save a cricket.
I spoke to her and said,
you and I
can always begin again.

She spins on,
her design ancient,
and I go back to folding clothes.

Before

4:11 and no hint
of first light.

A chirp
sharp, tentative
against the ocean's
ceaseless talk.

A chirp
small, scuttling
from a beetle whose custom
it is to sing
much later in the day
a tired tune that reminds us
of nothing so much
as heat
and dust.

A chirp
and he draws in
the sodden August night
and sings
thrilled
to find himself
here
before the day
asks anything at all
before the sun
before his God
with nothing but the singing.

Like a Cowboy, Shot from His Horse

Each rabbit had its own cage.
Breedings were arranged.

Mating was quick and matter-of-fact,
except for Blackbuck.

Put in with the chosen doe
he was nothing less
than a gentleman.

First they'd eat a little,
share a drink.
Maybe take the time
to chew a bit of hay.

Then he'd climb on.

And for 90 seconds his ass'd be
nipping and tucking
like a sewing machine needle.

Hair-raising speed,
eye-bulging concentration,
and the tip of his pink tongue,
flicking spittle on the doe's ears.

Then THUD.
He'd fall off, sideways,
like a cowboy,
shot from his horse.

First Steps

The house is silent
except for the ragged breathing
of the old cat.

I sigh,
startle myself
and the cat stops breathing
for not quite an eternity.

He's leaving me too.

I phone one son
after another,
hang up before the beep.

I could have left a message,

told each one,
how just this evening,
putting away the pot of chili
I won't finish in a month,
washing one cup, one bowl, one fork,

it came to me
that for thirty years I've been watching
first steps. Never once letting myself see
the slow dance,
the slick move away.

I want to say:
Turn back.
Crouch.
Find your balance.

Watch a moment.

I'm not sure I can do this
on my own.

Bus

There's no one on this bus
but me.

The woman in the seat behind,
her children asleep,
is already home,
the brother she hasn't seen for years,
pulling on pigtails that lie
wrapped in blue tissue paper
in her mother's cedar chest.

Her children are wherever
children go
when they sleep.

The man across the aisle is drunk,
cradles a bottle —
his ticket to anywhere
else.

At the very front a woman reads a magazine —
Are you good in bed?
She hasn't turned a page in hours.

The young couple at the back
are getting married on Saturday.
If they knew distance,
they might ask now
about return trips and lost luggage.

I wonder where you
would be
if you were here?
Would you let this cold glass
the rough upholstery,
hold you
keep you
from exits and little ecstasies.

Planting Spring

Yesterday I pulled winter
from the very back
of my closet:
boots, jackets, half
pairs of mitts.

Today I planted spring:
windflowers, moonlight,
glory of snow, angelica,
Miranda,
blue parrot, Texas flame —
as near to hope
as I dare.

How many women
I wonder
have knelt
this close to winter
a dark promise
beneath their nails.

I lean back,
run a hand down
the aching muscles
of my right side,
buttocks, thigh
and see all along the row
of houses,
other women
stretching
past winter.

But you, my friend,
keep your hands
buried,
do not lift your head.

Not even when I call your name.

Spring,
I am made to understand today,
will not come to everyone.

Pockets Full of Rotten Oranges

The men say Babe is wacko. She hates them.

We do okay, Babe and me. We have a twisted understanding. I say calm down, you old fart. She farts and calms down.

Babe loves oranges. Most horses don't.

I know when Babe has something on her mind. Her heart's crazy staccato, then the click of the bit and me, well-trained, I lay my head on the left side of her neck, out of her mane and hold on. She runs us through electric fence, the neighbour's sheep, the half-cracked barn door just to make sure I'm paying attention.

Babe doesn't like water. Won't stand still for rain. Smell of a puddle and I'm sitting on half a ton of black jello.

Buckets are okay and twice everyday I carry four of them, full of hot water, to ease the aching in her legs. Been doing it for years. Still the men can't get easy with the sight of Babe in buckets.

Front feet are easy. Babe steps in. Bit of friggin' to get the back ones right. She's boggy in the hocks so it hurts.

Babe settles. I light a smoke, sit under her belly to keep an eye on things. The men think I'm crazy as Babe for sitting there.

Only once I was too tired and wished her dead.

Took three days to get a back-hoe.

The men side-stepped her body easy and went on with their chores.

Me? I stood around, grounded. Watching Babe's eyes gather dust.

Rearview Mirror

There is always the thin black pup
crossing the highway
just ahead,
his dame four lanes over
her teats dripping.
And no matter all the times
I don't hit him,
the end of the story
remains
as inevitable
as this day ending
in disappointment
my mother in the passenger seat
reading
about all she could see firsthand
if she raised her head.

I refuse only the rearview.
Never mind
that the mirror
plays out
every black ending
whether I watch or not.

I have learned
that not looking back
saves me.

Such a small lesson
for a lifetime.

When will I learn
to expect the other black dog
the one that skirts my dreams
nipping at sleep
dragging the covers
from my eyes
forcing me to watch.
And watch again
his miserable and unremarkable death
on the long straight highway
from somewhere I don't remember
to nowhere at all.

The Scattering

The mare strangled in the night.

Early morning crows ate her eyes
and wedges of her tongue.
I harnessed the colt
and he dragged her,
raw-eyed,
up the new woods road.

I left her there,
above ground,
a banquet in the quiet clearing.

A year to the day
the dog brought home a leg.
I was desperate
to return it,
confirm the bare bones.

Expecting only the shape of her,
picked white
and settled slightly in the earth
I was not ready for the disarray,
the scattering.
So little remained,
a jaw,
a hip,
a small shelter of rib.

And one tooth,
found in my pocket
next laundry day.

The Smells of Clover

I remember days
framed neatly
between milkings.

The yellow warmth and sudden
safety of the low-ceilinged shed.
The cow's gentle chewing,
the haven of her flank
and the comfort of my cheek
pressed there. My hands,
warmed in my armpits.

Her moist popcorn breath
mixed with the smells
of clover and manure
and milk
thundering into the pail.

Eleven calves,
countless buckets of milk,
slabs of cheese, butter.
And finally the boxes of her flesh
brought late in the evening
on the back of a pickup.

I stay up until 4 a.m.
wrapping,
freezing,
smoking
one cigarette after another
to ease the sweet dark air
of blood.

Memory Train

Heroines in a movie,
my cousin and I,
until her little sister
peed her pants.

Walking the tracks
above their house,
too busy
being grand ladies
to watch out for Alice.
Her new white sandal
disappearing, her thin brown leg
following,
catching
beneath the rail.

We are forty years older
when we sit after breakfast
and I remember it
that way.
I can still see
Aunt Leona below us
on the veranda
wiping her hands.
Almost screaming.
And bits of sand jumping up
off the rails.
The train.
And Alice,
peeing.

Aunt Leona recalls only house and porch,
the tracks a long way off.
My cousin remembers nothing,
says it never happened, *Did it Alice?*
Did it Alice?

No, of course not, says Alice
who tells us
she has always been afraid
of trains.

Her Own Strength

Standing in her garden
two counties away,
she feels the old barn fall.

The morning's work almost
behind her — goat's beard, lobelia, lady's mantle —
she's arranged it all

to please herself. Crouched now,
arms deep in earth,
she begins the slow and steady pull

to free the thistle that once grew
beside the barn. She feels the earth
press against her bare feet

taking back 100 years of dust and voices.
Hears her patient pacing stall
to stall, waiting for the old horse,

the last of her beloved creatures, to die.
She's forgotten how deep things run,
her own strength. And now

the broken spade, the severed root,
the shadow of the barn
sliding down the sky one last time.

Stones

What if you could look up
and see tragedy
gathering
outside your kitchen window
or just ahead of you
in the line for coffee,
on what you had pegged
as a Monday
just like last
and the one before that?

What if you could look back
along the spine of your days,
see the moment
the pebble left your hand?

Would you quiet the ripples
until in a slow reversing arc
the stone lies once more
against your palm?

What would you erase?

Would you choose
the safer longing
of all you'll never have
to lose?

The only measure of your days, this pocket
full of stone.

All the Way Over

An old horse
an old woman,
the mare boggy in the hocks,
me the knees.
A difference too small to dwell on.

Her whole life
and the biggest part of mine
driven by the same demon,
his empty, fisted hands
one long demand
on us both.

He's gone now.

The mare never asked for anything
and I only asked the once
— white eyelet curtains.

He beat me 'til I couldn't stand.
The mare went without water that day,
but every other early morning
I've entered the barn,
loosed her from her stall,
and her skin all a twitch
she'd walk out into the paddock
and roll.

Always buy a horse that rolls
all the way over.
And she did. Over and over again
while I filled the water trough.

She hasn't rolled for years.
These days she stands and waits
in good weather in a patch of sun
or in bad she watches
from the open barn door.

Water ready, she comes for it,
drinks deep and long
her eyes closing softly
when she's had almost enough.

That's when I'll do it.
One bullet.
End of the road.
Nice to die,
getting what you want.
She'll never know what hit her.

He didn't.

Tomorrow morning
an old horse,
an old woman,
a gun
and two bullets.

ABOUT THE AUTHOR

Pam Calabrese MacLean lives in Antigonish, Nova Scotia, where she works in the Library of St. Francis Xavier University. She is a mother, a grandmother, a poet and a playwright. Her first book of poetry, *Twenty-four Names for Mother,* was published in 2006 by The Paper Journey Press (Wake Forest, NC). Her flash fiction has appeared in two US anthologies: *Women Behaving Badly,* 2004, and *Blink,* 2006. The Ida-Mae Poems, which form part of this collection, are the basis of MacLean's first play, *Her Father's Barn,* which has garnered awards in Nova Scotia, Ontario and British Columbia. Several of the poems were filmed for the Comedy Network. "Her Father's Barn" is forthcoming in an anthology entitled *Strong Women* from Lupin Press. Poems from the section "On a Chair Outside the Living" have won several awards, including firsts from *Other Voices* and *Room.* "Dream Diner" aired on the CBC program Between the Covers in 2005. Since her first public reading tour in 1991, MacLean has been delighting audiences across Canada.